HAL LEONARD STUDENT PIANO LIBRARY

BOOK 1 • ELEMENTARY / LATE ELEMENTARY

Piano Recital Showcase

FESTIVAL GEMS

10 NFMC SELECTED SOLOS

ISBN 978-1-4950-7234-5

7777 W. BLUEMOUND RD. P.O. BOX 13819 MILWAUKEE, WI 53213

In Australia Contact:
Hal Leonard Australia Pty. Ltd.
4 Lentara Court
Cheltenham, Victoria, 3192 Australia
Email: ausadmin@halleonard.com.au

Visit Hal Leonard Online at
www.halleonard.com

CONTENTS

Brooklyn's Waltz

To Brooklyn Hooper

Phillip Keveren

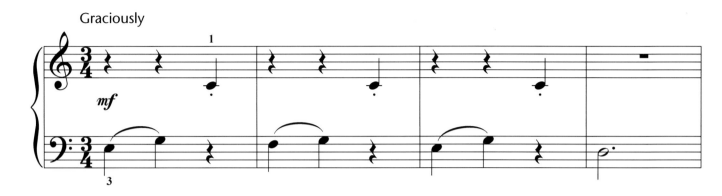

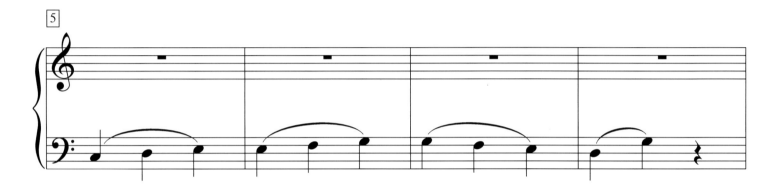

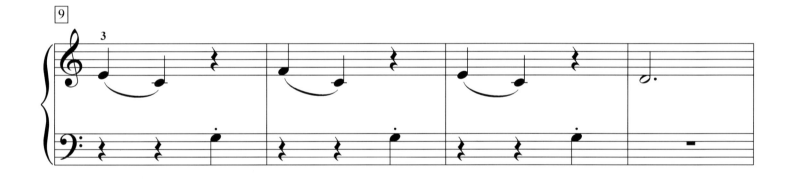

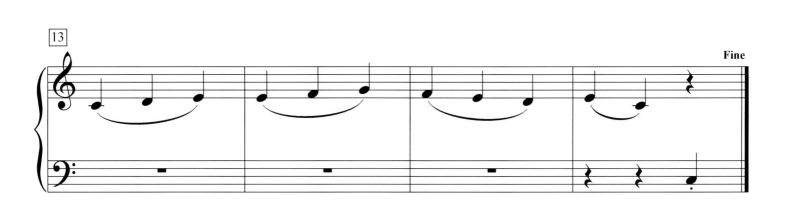

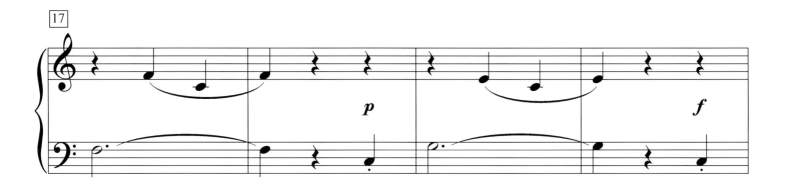

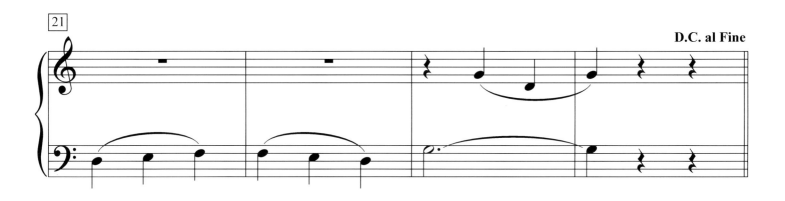

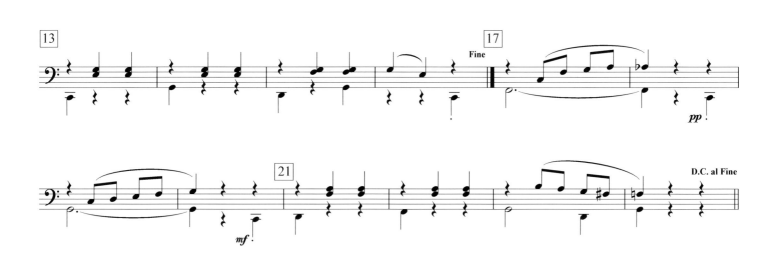

Feelin' Happy

Words and Music by
Mona Rejino

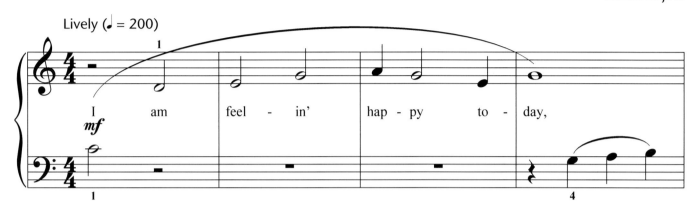

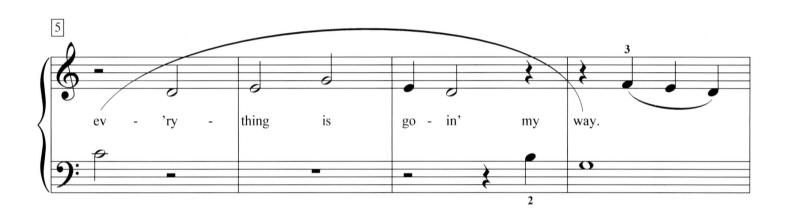

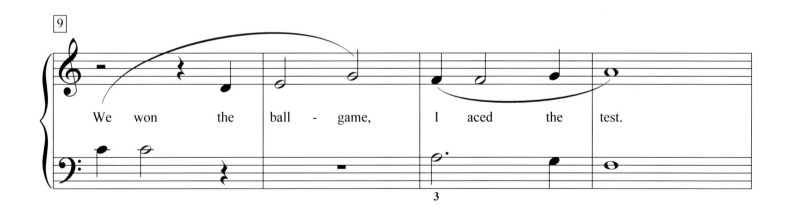

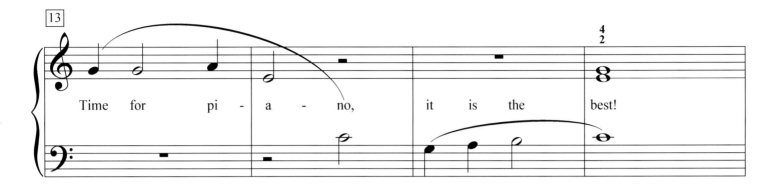

Time for pi - a - no, it is the best!

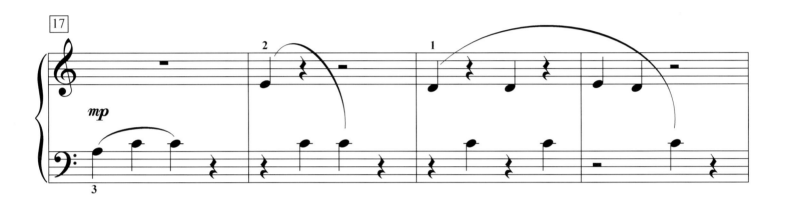

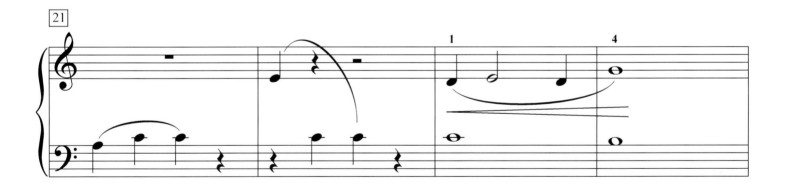

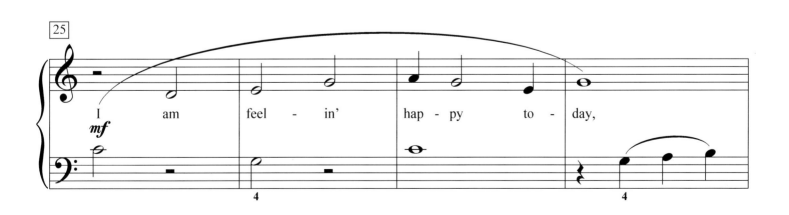

I am feel - in' hap - py to - day,

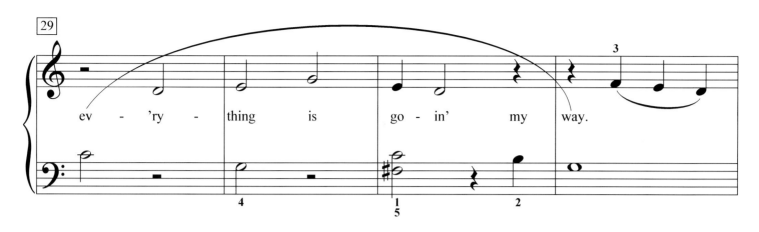

ev - 'ry - thing is go - in' my way.

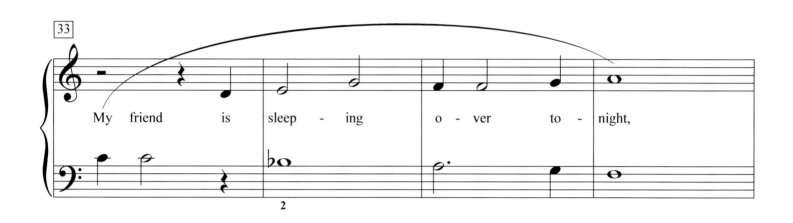

My friend is sleep - ing o - ver to - night,

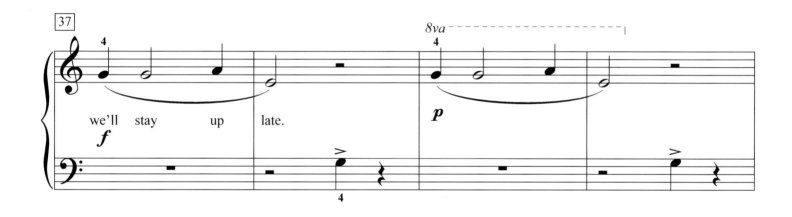

we'll stay up late.

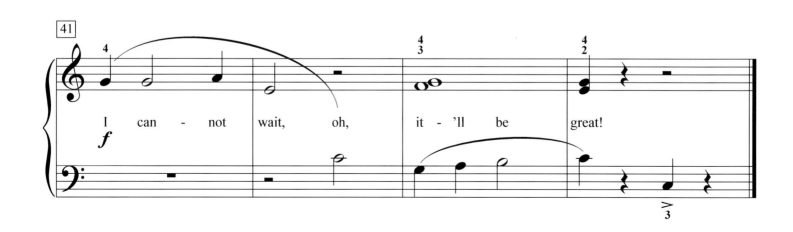

I can - not wait, oh, it - 'll be great!

New Orleans Jamboree

By Bill Boyd

Quickly (♩ = 160)

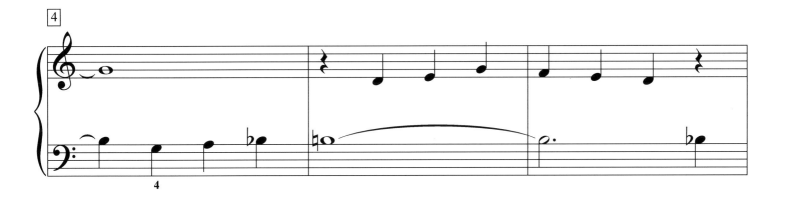

10

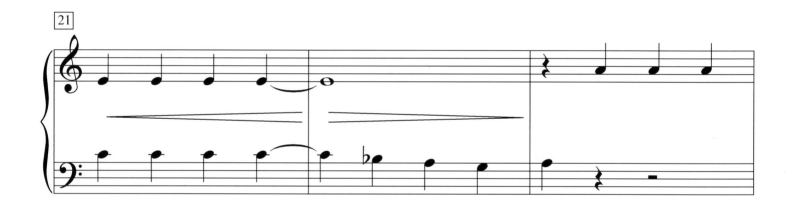

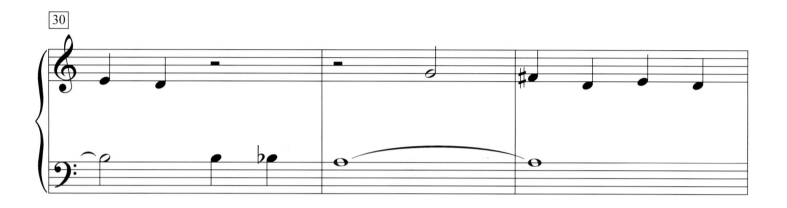

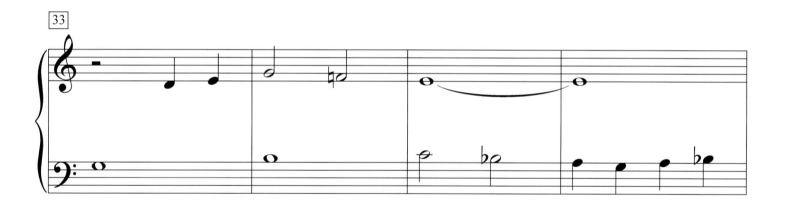

Pepperoni Pizza

Mona Rejino

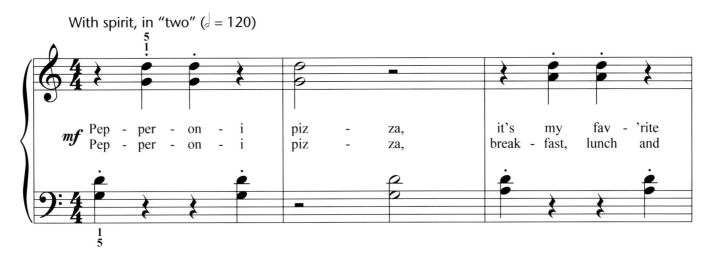

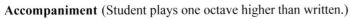

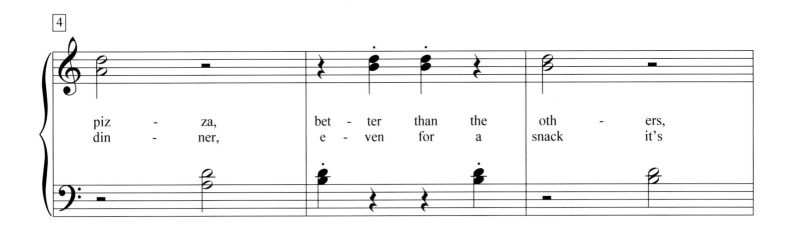

Accompaniment (Student plays one octave higher than written.)

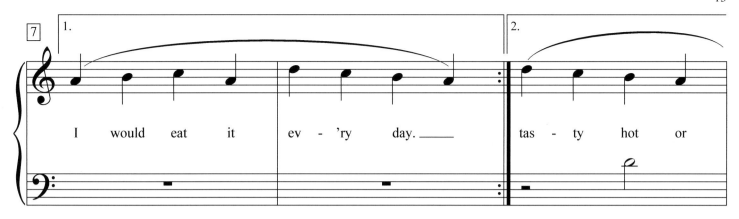

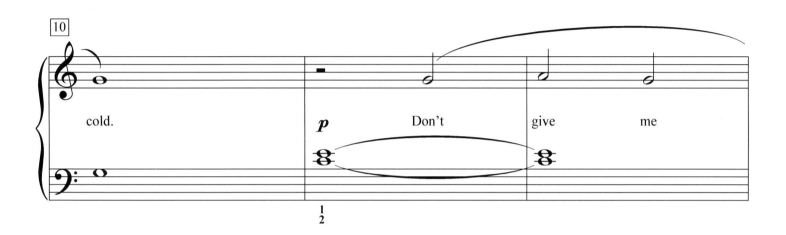

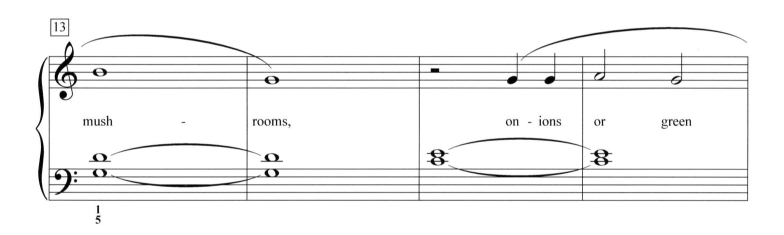

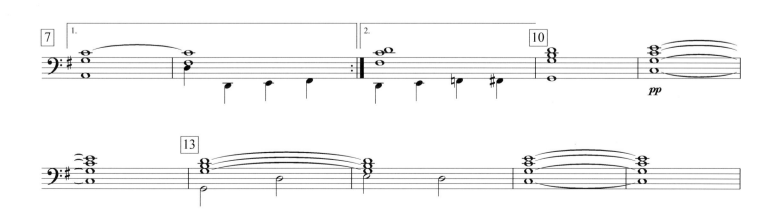

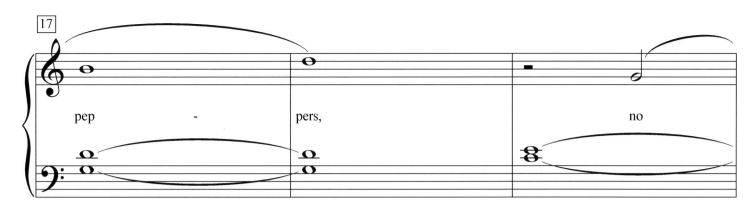

pep - pers,   no

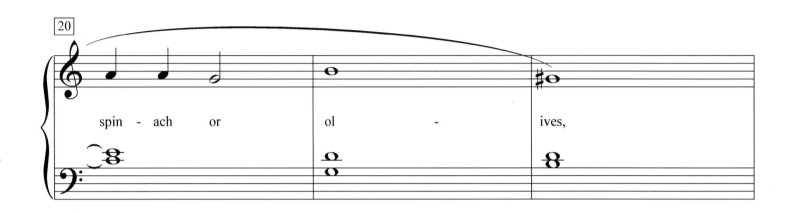

spin - ach or ol - ives,

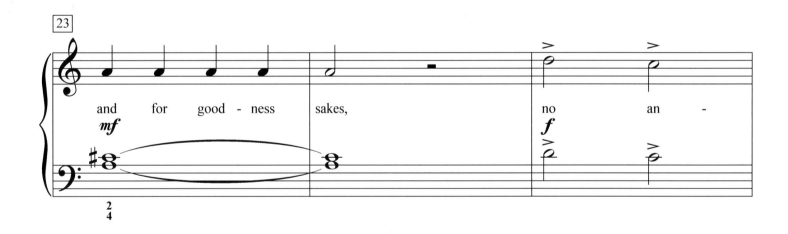

and for good - ness sakes,   no an -

mf   *f*

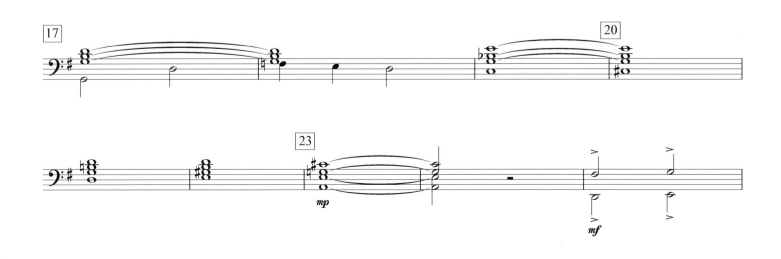

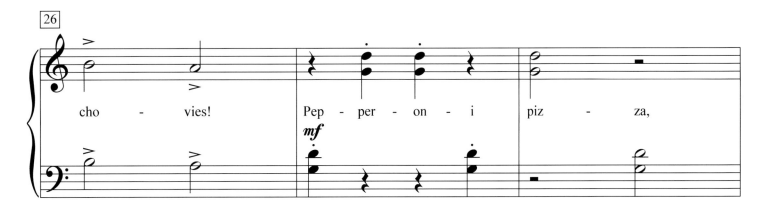

cho - vies! Pep - per - on - i piz - za,

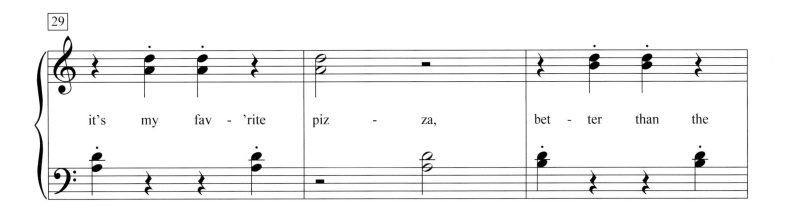

it's my fav - 'rite piz - za, bet - ter than the

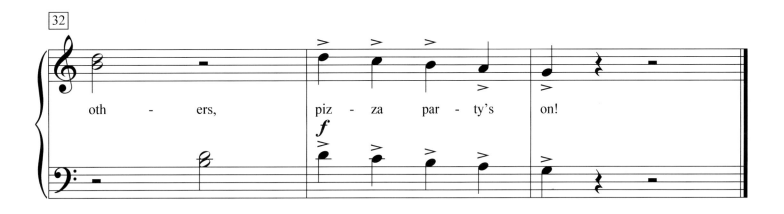

oth - ers, piz - za par - ty's on!

Things That Go Bump in the Night

By Carol Klose

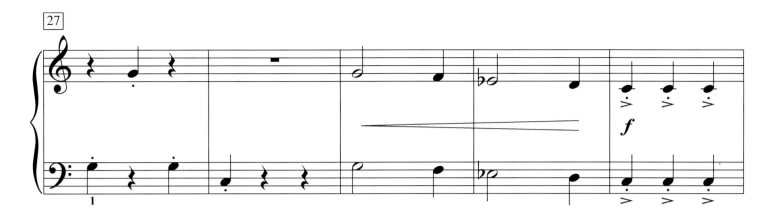

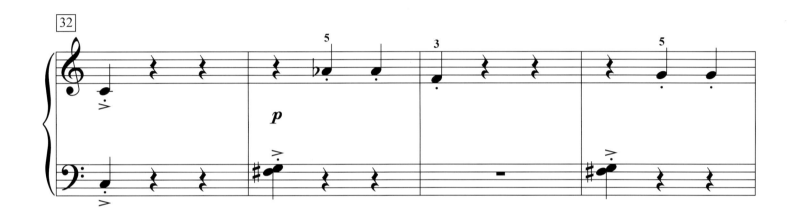

Very low chord cluster, slap with palm.

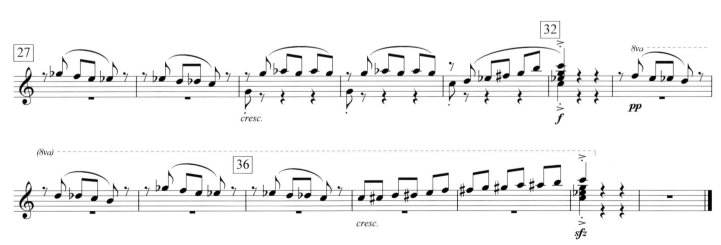

Chimichanga Cha-Cha

By Jennifer Linn

Moderately spicy (♩ = 200)

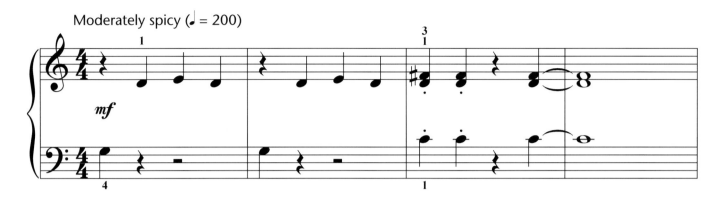

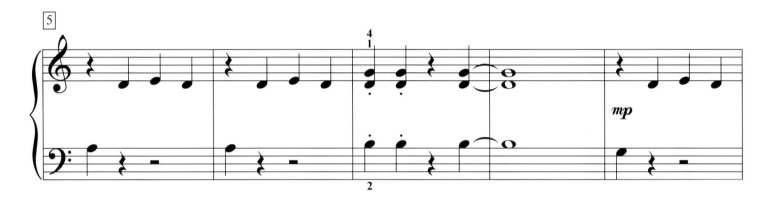

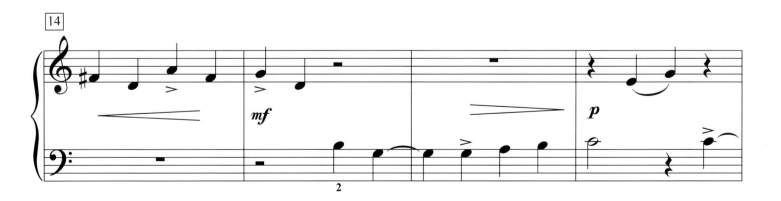

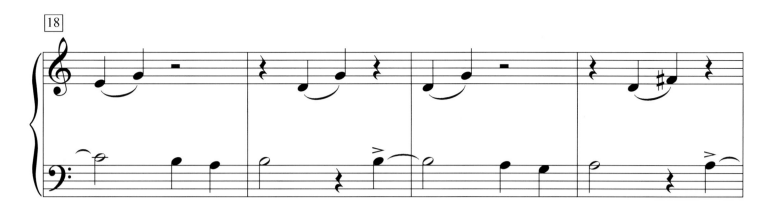

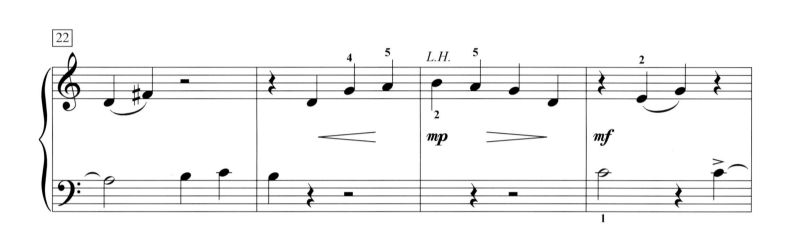

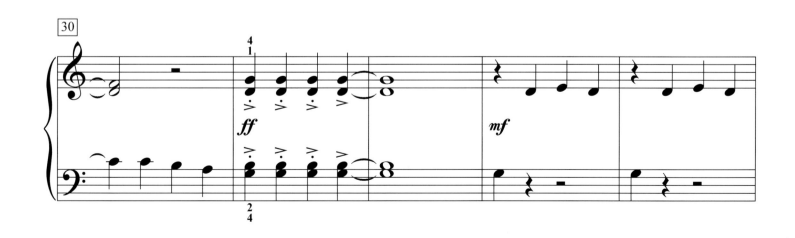

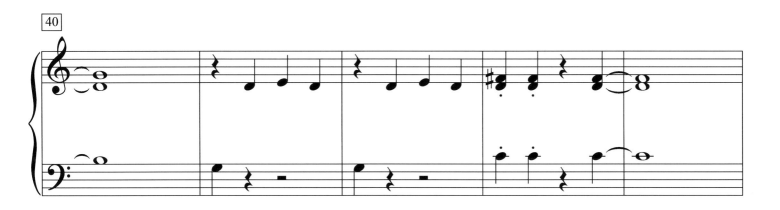

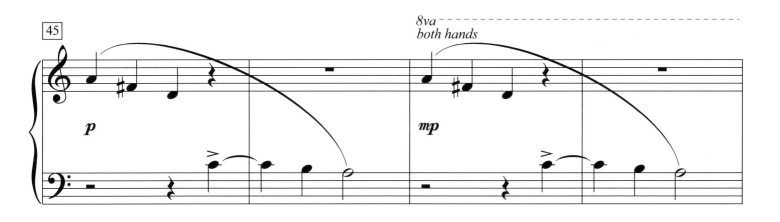

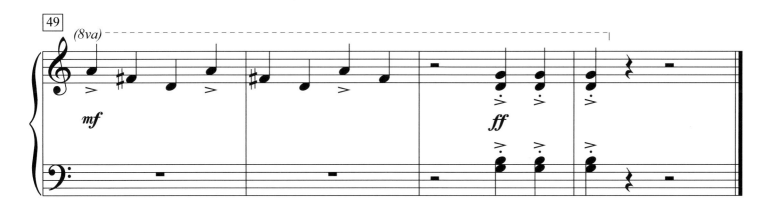

Lazy Daisy

By Jennifer and Mike Watts

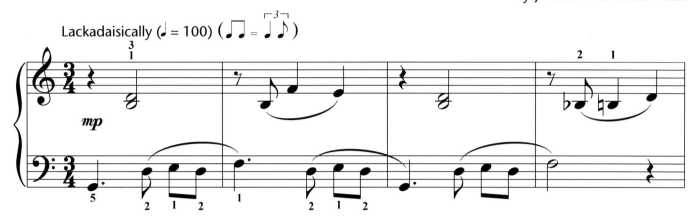

PBJ Blues

Words and Music by
Carol Klose

Jaunty Blues tempo (Swing 8ths) (♩ = 84)

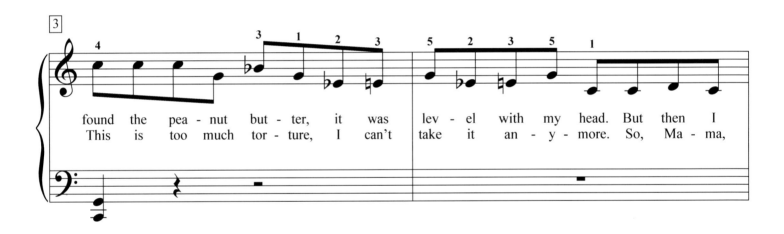

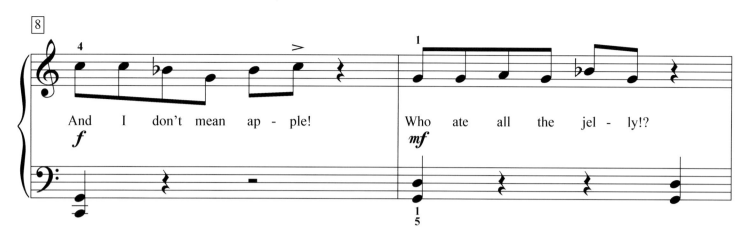

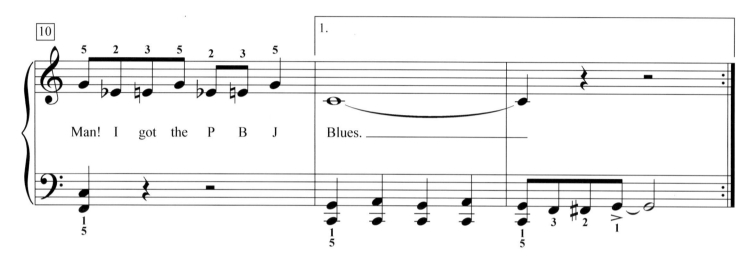

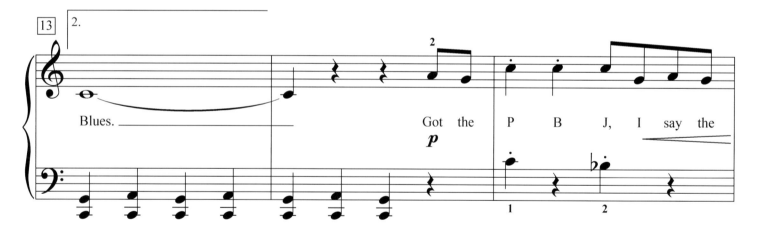

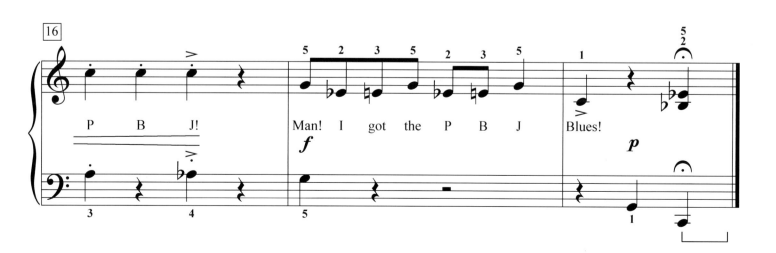

Sneakin' Cake
(But not before dinner!)

By Jennifer and Mike Watts

Tempo de Yummy (♩ = 140)

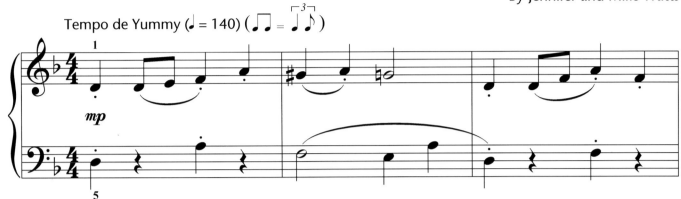

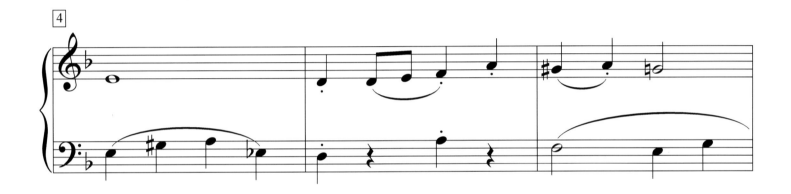

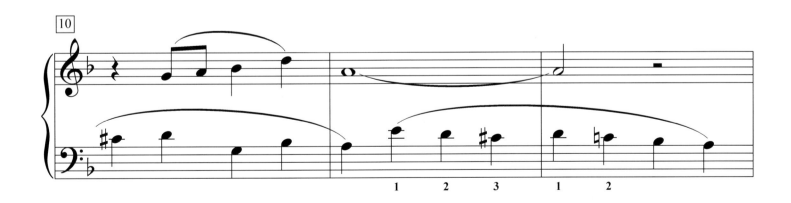

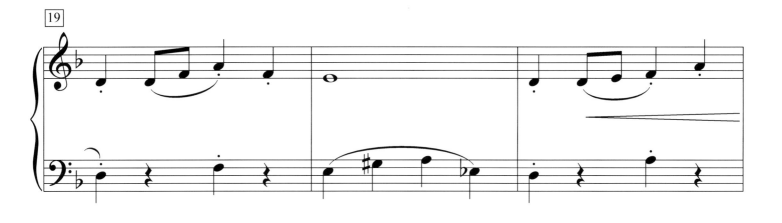

Footprints in the Snow

Future wish to know,
pure impatience.
Footprints in the snow,
peaceful presence.

By Jennifer Linn

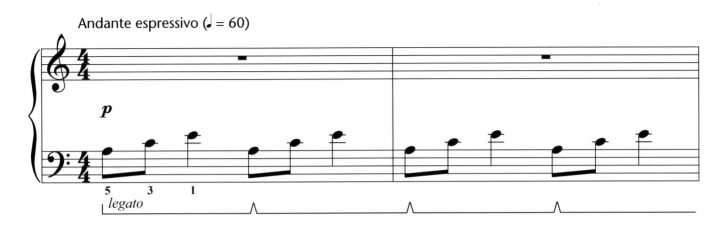

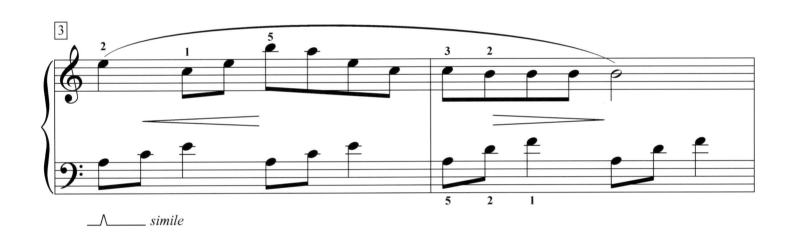

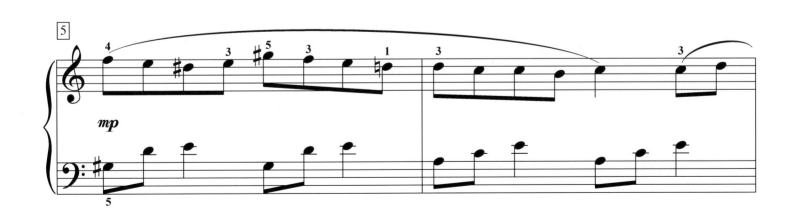

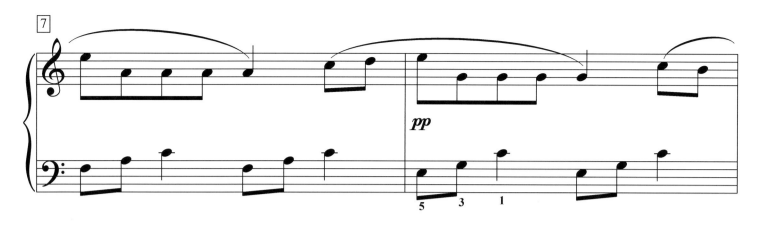

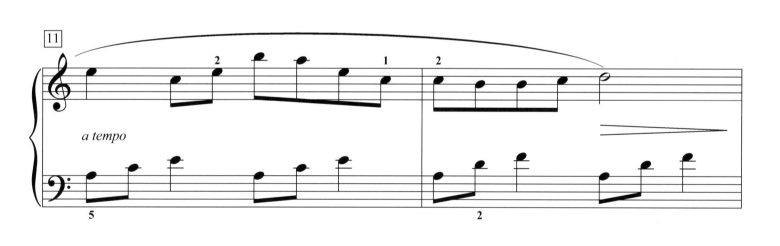

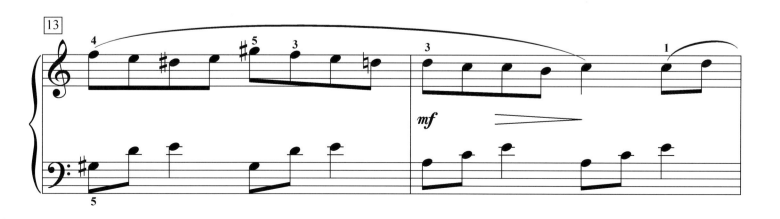

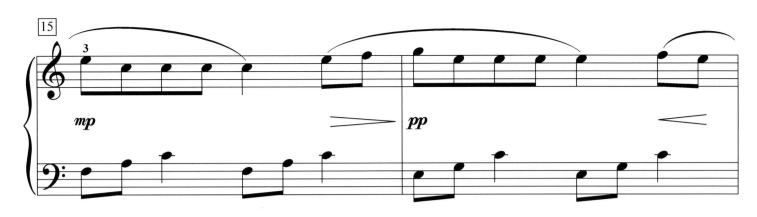

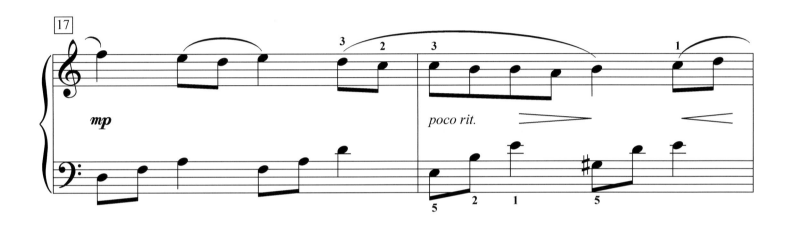

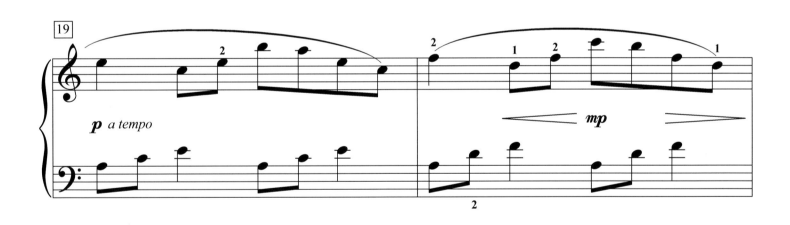

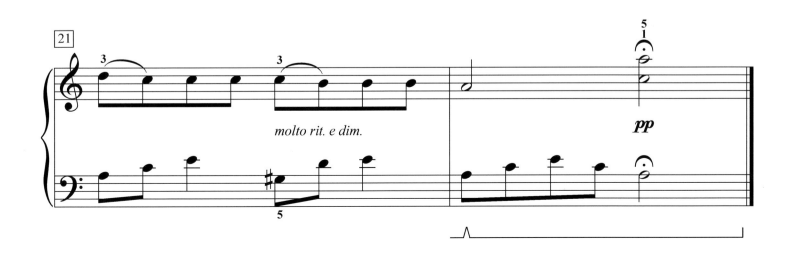

COMPOSER SHOWCASE
HAL LEONARD STUDENT PIANO LIBRARY

This series showcases great original piano music from our **Hal Leonard Student Piano Library** family of composers. Carefully graded for easy selection.

BILL BOYD

JAZZ BITS (AND PIECES)
Early Intermediate Level
00290312 11 Solos......................$7.99

JAZZ DELIGHTS
Intermediate Level
00240435 11 Solos......................$8.99

JAZZ FEST
Intermediate Level
00240436 10 Solos......................$8.99

JAZZ PRELIMS
Early Elementary Level
00290032 12 Solos......................$7.99

JAZZ SKETCHES
Intermediate Level
00220001 8 Solos......................$8.99

JAZZ STARTERS
Elementary Level
00290425 10 Solos......................$8.99

JAZZ STARTERS II
Late Elementary Level
00290434 11 Solos......................$7.99

JAZZ STARTERS III
Late Elementary Level
00290465 12 Solos......................$8.99

THINK JAZZ!
Early Intermediate Level
00290417 Method Book............$12.99

TONY CARAMIA

JAZZ MOODS
Intermediate Level
00296728 8 Solos......................$6.95

SUITE DREAMS
Intermediate Level
00296775 4 Solos......................$6.99

SONDRA CLARK

DAKOTA DAYS
Intermediate Level
00296521 5 Solos......................$6.95

FLORIDA FANTASY SUITE
Intermediate Level
00296766 3 Duets......................$7.95

THREE ODD METERS
Intermediate Level
00296472 3 Duets......................$6.95

MATTHEW EDWARDS

CONCERTO FOR YOUNG PIANISTS
FOR 2 PIANOS, FOUR HANDS
Intermediate Level Book/CD
00296356 3 Movements $19.99

CONCERTO NO. 2 IN G MAJOR
FOR 2 PIANOS, 4 HANDS
Intermediate Level Book/CD
00296670 3 Movements............$17.99

PHILLIP KEVEREN

MOUSE ON A MIRROR
Late Elementary Level
00296361 5 Solos......................$8.99

MUSICAL MOODS
Elementary/Late Elementary Level
00296714 7 Solos......................$6.99

SHIFTY-EYED BLUES
Late Elementary Level
00296374 5 Solos......................$7.99

CAROL KLOSE

THE BEST OF CAROL KLOSE
Early to Late Intermediate Level
00146151 15 Solos....................$12.99

CORAL REEF SUITE
Late Elementary Level
00296354 7 Solos......................$7.50

DESERT SUITE
Intermediate Level
00296667 6 Solos......................$7.99

FANCIFUL WALTZES
Early Intermediate Level
00296473 5 Solos......................$7.95

GARDEN TREASURES
Late Intermediate Level
00296787 5 Solos......................$8.50

ROMANTIC EXPRESSIONS
Intermediate to Late Intermediate Level
00296923 5 Solos......................$8.99

WATERCOLOR MINIATURES
Early Intermediate Level
00296848 7 Solos......................$7.99

JENNIFER LINN

AMERICAN IMPRESSIONS
Intermediate Level
00296471 6 Solos......................$8.99

ANIMALS HAVE FEELINGS TOO
Early Elementary/Elementary Level
00147789 8 Solos......................$8.99

AU CHOCOLAT
Late Elementary/Early Intermediate Level
00298110 7 Solos......................$8.99

CHRISTMAS IMPRESSIONS
Intermediate Level
00296706 8 Solos......................$8.99

JUST PINK
Elementary Level
00296722 9 Solos......................$8.99

LES PETITES IMAGES
Late Elementary Level
00296664 7 Solos......................$8.99

LES PETITES IMPRESSIONS
Intermediate Level
00296355 6 Solos......................$8.99

REFLECTIONS
Late Intermediate Level
00296843 5 Solos......................$8.99

TALES OF MYSTERY
Intermediate Level
00296769 6 Solos......................$8.99

LYNDA LYBECK-ROBINSON

ALASKA SKETCHES
Early Intermediate Level
00119637 8 Solos......................$8.99

AN AWESOME ADVENTURE
Late Elementary Level
00137563 8 Solos......................$7.99

FOR THE BIRDS
Early Intermediate/Intermediate Level
00237078 9 Solos......................$8.99

WHISPERING WOODS
Late Elementary Level
00275905 9 Solos......................$8.99

MONA REJINO

CIRCUS SUITE
Late Elementary Level
00296665 5 Solos......................$8.99

COLOR WHEEL
Early Intermediate Level
00201951 6 Solos......................$9.99

IMPRESIONES DE ESPAÑA
Intermediate Level
00337520 6 Solos......................$8.99

IMPRESSIONS OF NEW YORK
Intermediate Level
00364212......................$8.99

JUST FOR KIDS
Elementary Level
00296840 8 Solos......................$7.99

MERRY CHRISTMAS MEDLEYS
Intermediate Level
00296799 5 Solos......................$8.99

MINIATURES IN STYLE
Intermediate Level
00148088 6 Solos......................$8.99

PORTRAITS IN STYLE
Early Intermediate Level
00296507 6 Solos......................$8.99

EUGÉNIE ROCHEROLLE

CELEBRATION SUITE
Intermediate Level
00152724 3 Duets......................$8.99

ENCANTOS ESPAÑOLES (SPANISH DELIGHTS)
Intermediate Level
00125451 6 Solos......................$8.99

JAMBALAYA
Intermediate Level
00296654 2 Pianos, 8 Hands.....$12.99
00296725 2 Pianos, 4 Hands.......$7.95

JEROME KERN CLASSICS
Intermediate Level
00296577 10 Solos....................$12.99

LITTLE BLUES CONCERTO
Early Intermediate Level
00142801 2 Pianos, 4 Hands......$12.99

TOUR FOR TWO
Late Elementary Level
00296832 6 Duets......................$9.99

TREASURES
Late Elementary/Early Intermediate Level
00296924 7 Solos......................$8.99

JEREMY SISKIND

BIG APPLE JAZZ
Intermediate Level
00278209 8 Solos......................$8.99

MYTHS AND MONSTERS
Late Elementary/Early Intermediate Level
00148148 9 Solos......................$8.99

CHRISTOS TSITSAROS

DANCES FROM AROUND THE WORLD
Early Intermediate Level
00296688 7 Solos......................$8.99

FIVE SUMMER PIECES
Late Intermediate/Advanced Level
00361235 5 Solos....................$12.99

LYRIC BALLADS
Intermediate/Late Intermediate Level
00102404 6 Solos......................$8.99

POETIC MOMENTS
Intermediate Level
00296403 8 Solos......................$8.99

SEA DIARY
Early Intermediate Level
00253486 9 Solos......................$8.99

SONATINA HUMORESQUE
Late Intermediate Level
00296772 3 Movements............$6.99

SONGS WITHOUT WORDS
Intermediate Level
00296506 9 Solos......................$9.99

THREE PRELUDES
Early Advanced Level
00130747 3 Solos......................$8.99

THROUGHOUT THE YEAR
Late Elementary Level
00296723 12 Duets....................$6.95

ADDITIONAL COLLECTIONS

AT THE LAKE
by Elvina Pearce
Elementary/Late Elementary Level
00131642 10 Solos and Duets.....$7.99

CHRISTMAS FOR TWO
by Dan Fox
Early Intermediate Level
00290069 13 Duets....................$8.99

CHRISTMAS JAZZ
by Mike Springer
Intermediate Level
00296525 6 Solos......................$8.99

COUNTY RAGTIME FESTIVAL
by Fred Kern
Intermediate Level
00296882 7 Solos......................$7.99

LITTLE JAZZERS
by Jennifer Watts
Elementary/Late Elementary Level
00154573 9 Solos......................$8.99

PLAY THE BLUES!
by Luann Carman
Early Intermediate Level
00296357 10 Solos....................$9.99

ROLLER COASTERS & RIDES
by Jennifer & Mike Watts
Intermediate Level
00131144 8 Duets......................$8.99

www.halleonard.com

Prices, contents, and availability subject to change without notice.

0321
144

Hal Leonard Student Piano Library

The Hal Leonard Student Piano Library has great music and solid pedagogy delivered in a truly creative and comprehensive method. It's that simple. A creative approach to learning using solid pedagogy and the best music produces skilled musicians! Great music means motivated students, inspired teachers and delighted parents. It's a method that encourages practice, progress, confidence, and best of all – success.

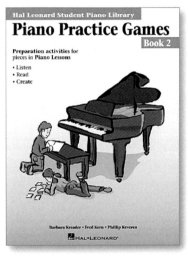

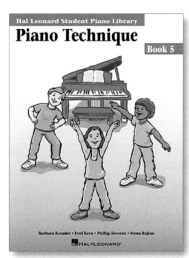

PIANO LESSONS BOOK 1
00296177 Book/Online Audio............................ $9.99
00296001 Book Only.. $7.99

PIANO PRACTICE GAMES BOOK 1
00296002 .... $7.99

PIANO SOLOS BOOK 1
00296568 Book/Online Audio............................ $9.99
00296003 Book Only.. $7.99

PIANO THEORY WORKBOOK BOOK 1
00296023 .... $7.50

PIANO TECHNIQUE BOOK 1
00296563 Book/Online Audio............................ $8.99
00296105 Book Only.. $7.99

NOTESPELLER FOR PIANO BOOK 1
00296088 .... $7.99

TEACHER'S GUIDE BOOK 1
00296048 .... $7.99

PIANO LESSONS BOOK 2
00296178 Book/Online Audio............................ $9.99
00296006 Book Only.. $7.99

PIANO PRACTICE GAMES BOOK 2
00296007 .... $8.99

PIANO SOLOS BOOK 2
00296569 Book/Online Audio............................ $8.99
00296008 Book Only.. $7.99

PIANO THEORY WORKBOOK BOOK 2
00296024 .... $7.99

PIANO TECHNIQUE BOOK 2
00296564 Book/Online Audio............................ $8.99
00296106 Book Only.. $7.99

NOTESPELLER FOR PIANO BOOK 2
00296089 .... $6.99

PIANO LESSONS BOOK 3
00296179 Book/Online Audio............................ $9.99
00296011 Book Only.. $7.99

PIANO PRACTICE GAMES BOOK 3
00296012 .... $7.99

PIANO SOLOS BOOK 3
00296570 Book/Online Audio............................ $8.99
00296013 Book Only.. $7.99

PIANO THEORY WORKBOOK BOOK 3
00296025 .... $7.99

PIANO TECHNIQUE BOOK 3
00296565 Book/Enhanced CD Pack.................. $8.99
00296114 Book Only.. $7.99

NOTESPELLER FOR PIANO BOOK 3
00296167 .... $7.99

PIANO LESSONS BOOK 4
00296180 Book/Online Audio............................ $9.99
00296026 Book Only.. $7.99

PIANO PRACTICE GAMES BOOK 4
00296027 .... $6.99

PIANO SOLOS BOOK 4
00296571 Book/Online Audio............................ $8.99
00296028 Book Only.. $7.99

PIANO THEORY WORKBOOK BOOK 4
00296038 .... $7.99

PIANO TECHNIQUE BOOK 4
00296566 Book/Online Audio............................ $8.99
00296115 Book Only.. $7.99

PIANO LESSONS BOOK 5
00296181 Book/Online Audio............................ $9.99
00296041 Book Only.. $8.99

PIANO SOLOS BOOK 5
00296572 Book/Online Audio............................ $9.99
00296043 Book Only.. $7.99

PIANO THEORY WORKBOOK BOOK 5
00296042 .... $8.99

PIANO TECHNIQUE BOOK 5
00296567 Book/Online Audio............................ $8.99
00296116 Book Only.. $8.99

ALL-IN-ONE PIANO LESSONS
00296761 Book A – Book/Online Audio $10.99
00296776 Book B – Book/Online Audio $10.99
00296851 Book C – Book/Online Audio $10.99
00296852 Book D – Book/Online Audio $10.99

Prices, contents, and availability subject to change without notice.

www.halleonard.com